# Hoodwinked III

*Town Hall: Code, the Debasing of America*

"WHEN JUST ONE OF US LOSES JUST ONE OF OUR RIGHTS, THEN THE FREEDOMS OF ALL OF US ARE DIMINISHED"

*— Robert Mueller,*
*Director of the FBI, under President Obama –*
*Special Prosecutor under President Trump*

# Hoodwinked III

## TOWN HALL:
### Code, the Debasing of America

◆

*The LittleHouse Diaries*
*2010 – 2013*

# HOODWINKED III

*The Illegal Taxation of Private American Homes*

### Vol. III
### TOWN HALL: Code, the Debasing of America

◆

*"Government of the Government,
By the Government,
For the Government."*

# J.A. PATRINA

ISBN: 978-1-7330672-3-2     [Paperback Edition]

Please visit *hoodwinked.net* for video versions of this manuscript.
Printed and bound in The United States of America.

Published by LittleHouse Enterprises Inc.

LittleHouse
ENTERPRISES

The LittleHouse Diaries
2010 – 2013

TOWN HALL

*Code, the Debasing of America*

J.A. PATRINA

"WHEN TOWN AUTHORITIES CAN PLAY RECKLESS GAMES WITH
THEIR RESIDENTS, ABUSE THE LAW AT MANY LEVELS — GOING AS FAR
AS DECEIVING JUDGES - AND EXPECT TO GET AWAY WITH IT ... WE ALL
HAVE A PROBLEM".

*— The LittleHouse Diaries 2010 – 2013*

# The Hoodwinked Books

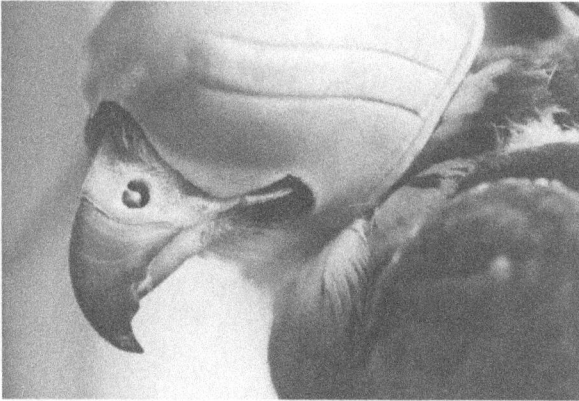

There are Three (3) "Hoodwinked" books authored by Joe Patrina, the first constitutionally oriented, the second historically oriented, the third personally oriented.

Within these separate orientations, the books explore the natural and constitutional rights to private property held by all American citizens. This book, *Volume III – Town Hall*, recounts illegal search and seizure measures taken by my local government violating one's rights to private property. These violations continued for three years until finally dying down. This is a "behind the scenes" look at how far government overreach has gotten to in the modern socialist era.

- *Hoodwinked Volume I – Constitutional Issues*

- *Hoodwinked Volume II – The Arc of Land Ownership Rights from Old England to 1620 Plymouth, to the American Revolution, to Modern Times*

- *Hoodwinked Volume III – TOWN HALL – Code, the Debasing of America*

# About The Author

*Joe Patrina* is an American singer/songwriter based in Connecticut, where he leads the popular country/rock group LittleHouse. As with his songwriting, Joe applies his seasoned observational skills and to-the-point writing style to pen insightful works on sports, history, politics, medicine, music and law.

# The Garden —
# It Used to Be My Town, Too

*Above: Our actual" little house" home in Simsbury, Ct,
that I eventually named the band after.*

I grew up in Simsbury, Connecticut, one of the oldest and most blessed towns in the United States. In the 1960s, I picked shade tobacco in the same fields as had Martin Luther King Jr., a generation before me. I played sports on the town's wonderful baseball fields. I attended middle school in the building that is now Town Hall, and my class of 1970 was the first to go from 9th grade to 12th in the new high school.

During those years, I ran through the fields and meadows of this glorious Garden of Eden nestled in the Farmington River Valley. In 1978, at the age of 25, I moved my new wife and myself to Manhattan to forge a career. Our parents and our immediate family members stayed put in town, so we always came back, and indeed we never truly left Simsbury.

While living in NYC, my first wife died of cancer; I founded a company, remarried, saved some money, and, in 1991, bought a weekend house in West Simsbury. Now I was really back, even if for but a few days per week.

*My Family in 2010, before the onslaught*

In 2007 I retired and moved into the West Simsbury house for good. At heart a songwriter and musician, I soon organized a group of musicians hailing from distant parts of Connecticut. We tested our songs with audiences in the barn on my property; a songwriter's workshop, if you will.

The band, named "LittleHouse," grew competent, then better, then compelling. Everything progressed smoothly until I ventured out and decided to rent the town's outdoor stage in Simsbury Meadows, called the "Simsbury Performing Arts Center".

This engagement introduced me to Simsbury's new style of rule, a mentality, I soon learned, that retained none of the older, citizen-centric sensibilities of the town governments from my youth.

Instead, the First Selectman (the mayor) and the Fire Marshall did their best to run down my musical adventure. Although I am not a lawyer, it seemed to me that to do so, they probably stretched and even broke laws and all notions of common decency. And this assault continued for three years. I kept notes. The diary details.

# Spring 2010 —
# The Huckabee Factor

I might as well blame and credit everything you are about to read on an entertainment lawyer (and New York University professor), to whom I will fondly to here refer to as "Beanie," who maintains offices in Manhattan and Hackensack (go figure).

In early 2010, after a three-year period of writing upward of 100 songs and performing in the barn on my property, I itched to take things further with my band, *LittleHouse*, and I heard that with Beanie, I would really get the skinny on my chances.

"I listened to the CDs that you sent me and read your concept paper," Beanie opened as we started our four-hour meeting, "Great stuff, really, but so what?" he asks rhetorically.

For the next few hours "the Beanie Monster" rants that no one helps anyone in show business, that no Godfather or patron will champion my art, and that I will need to forge success strictly on my own, just as I had with Wall Street Systems, the software company I founded in 1987, which he had apparently researched.

Beanie: *"Do you know how to get to Carnegie Hall?"*

Joe: *"Practice?"*

"No, you rent it," he clarified. "Did anyone ever help you at Wall Street Systems?"

"Actually, we did have trouble with some of our employees, most of our customers, and all of our competitors," I joked.

"Well, this is a lot worse", he postulated, oblivious to my nuanced humor. "Back then you built a computer system *that the world actually needed; you helped manage the world's currency exchange, for God's sake. In show business, no one needs your music, even if it's good.*"

Gulp. Beanie was throwing body blows and they landed. Hard.

*"But you can do this"*, he reassured me, *"The music is compelling, and just as you did before, you have to plan and control everything yourself and make it all happen, otherwise forget it."*

What a motivator.

The gist of what we faced, according to Beanie: Rent stages and figure out how to sell a lot of tickets. Everything else? Mere detail. And the details, he assured me, were my problems, too.

*"You're an American, for heaven's sake,"* I remember him saying to me at some point.

I drove back from Beanie's in early 2010, motoring up Interstate 84 and thinking about the political fury all around. It was an election year with boatloads of governor, senate and house seats in play, with a lot of anti-Obama sentiment already building as ObamaCare progressed in the Democratically controlled House and Senate chambers. The Tea Party took shape, and drama hung in the air.

It dawned on me that politics consumed everyone, whereas no one cared about my band *LittleHouse*. Of course according to Beanie, no one would ever care about *LittleHouse* unless they could make easy and ready money off us.

As I neared my highway exit, it hit me ... do a show mixing politicians and bands ... on the same stage.

Between bands, the politicians could be interviewed on a couch - by a local radio personality, the way Bill Clinton appeared on the Arsenio Hall Show playing his saxophone. The politicians could display their human side and I could sell a lot of tickets. The bands, including *LittleHouse*, would serve as filler.

I named it "*The 2010 New England Music Festival*" or "*NEFest*" for short.

The next morning, I called the manager of the Performing Arts Center in Simsbury. He had already witnessed a *LittleHouse* rehearsal prior, knew the band, and had a good grasp on me.

I wanted to rent his Performing Arts Center stage, an outdoor masterpiece in Simsbury Meadows, owned by the Town of Simsbury, yet built by Tom Vincent, a former republican first selectman using private donations. The facility could handle an audience of as many as 8,000. It served as the early-summer home of the Hartford Symphony each year, but after June, became available for rent to various third party promoters to stage shows.

The manager and I met the next morning at the Starbucks in Simsbury. I explained my unique concept, and he said he would present it to the Performing Arts Committee (PAC).

Present it? I thought I was renting!

You see, as I already said, but you may have missed, the Town of Simsbury owns The Performing Arts Center. And this … this is <u>really</u> where our story begins.

After reviewing my application, which described the combined band/ politician format, the Performing Arts Committee (PAC) hemmed and hawed, but after a few meetings they decided to recommend the show, and I soon signed a site license agreement (a contract) with Mary, the town's First Selectman, the rough equivalent of a mayor. As such, I will refer to her as "The Mayor" or "Mayor Mary."

Next, The Hartford Symphony Box Office, which already sold tickets for their own concerts at that venue, agreed to sell my tickets at a $4 per ticket commission fee.

I then turned my attention to securing the bands and politicians.

The politicians themselves quickly expressed their interest. They got it. "Make me look cool, like Clinton." But the campaign managers grew wary. Things could backfire.

I soon learned that to discuss matters with a politician you could have meetings with them at their headquarters, or you could just show up in whatever town they were at that day and track them down. Politics is a street thing for sure.

Dannel Malloy, a Stamford Democrat and candidate for governor, met my project partner William Landers in Barkhamstead, Connecticut and said he wanted to do the show. Later, I met Malloy myself. At the time, I thought, ice water coursed Malloy's veins. He won as Governor.

Linda McMahon, a Republican running for Senate, the owner of a big show-business wrestling company, appeared inclined to sign up for our show, but then things suddenly went silent from within her camp. So I went down to Madison, Connecticut to catch her before Linda marched in their July 4th parade.

We chatted and she advised me on NEFest, saying I really needed a headliner to pull it all together, and that she knew a little bit about that kind of thing. *How about Mike Huckabee?* I posed (who ran in the Republican presidential primary of 2008 and by 2010 had a TV show on the FOX network).

Snapping her fingers and beaming her radiant blue eyes at me, she said, *You get Huckabee and everyone will be there.*

Once home, I tracked down Huckabee's agent. Over a few phone calls, I clarified the show's format, its date, and Mike's proposed stage time, and how the governor could make it from the city to Simsbury after his Saturday morning taping on FOX and subsequently find himself en route back to Arkansas that same night, on a flight path I researched.

We signed a personal appearance agreement (a contract).

I immediately began to let people know that NEFest now featured a potential president, governor, senator, and congressman, plus the four bands that I retained.

That's when I got "The Call."

*Joe, could you come down to Town Hall, the PAC (Performing Arts Committee) would like to ask you a few questions...*

An American Rock Band
LittleHouse

# Summer 2010 —
# The Democrat Town Committee

This meeting, called a few weeks before the NEFest date, proved just the beginning of an all-out assault intended to kill the show.

Suddenly, the committee that already approved the show …. asked me to reappear before it, despite the existence of a contract executed with Mary ("The Mayor"), a contract upon which I already made other financial arrangements with bands and suppliers, not to mention Huckabee's fee (don't ask).

Not wanting to fight city hall, I agreed to come down, accompanied by my lawyer, an "old school" Democrat BTW, just in case.

I arrived at Town Hall in the early evening, and sat at the table with the committee, looking around at all the strangers' faces that packed the room wanting to witness what came next.

Suddenly, a man who I did not recognize stood, and started speaking in angry, accusative tones. He pointed to another man sitting in the back, identifying him as the head of the Democratic Town Committee.

*Fine,* I said.

Then the official challenge began. It opened with the aggressive charge that I had deceived the town. The angry man claimed that earlier, when I first appeared before the committee, I had proposed an *"entertainment" event, which turned out to be a Tea Party political rally in disguise.*

*Furthermore,* he continued, *it was not appropriate to use town property for political purposes… and,* he insisted, *your political language in the ads such as*

*'God and America' and 'Traditional American Families' should not be mentioned in municipal venues.*

And so, therefore, he concluded, *...because of this deception, you operated fraudulently, and in doing so, the contract that you entered into with the Town of Simsbury is null and void.*

Wow. Those were a lot of objections.

My internal reaction conjured Major Wolfgang Hochstetter from the old TV sitcom "Hogan's Heroes" when he would scream "Who eeeeees theees man?" I guess I was the Hogan figure, but in my mind I was also saying, "Really, who *is* this guy?"

Similar to Hogan's Gestapo adversary, this fellow exhibited perpetual anger, and, similar to a good Nazi working with his SD adjunct, he had the Democratic Town Committee chief by his side.

I could not imagine that Democrat party people had any authority to lord over the Performing Arts Counsel, a town government entity, yet it must have been arranged, as it was indeed happening.

But I was calm, and naively, I looked forward to painting the true picture of the show to demonstrate that his fears of my alleged deceptive nature held no ground. I felt sure I could win him over.

First things first, which meant squashing the fraud stuff. In the legal world, fraud is verboten.

To achieve this, everyone received a copy of the original application I submitted weeks earlier, which included a typed overview of the show I envisioned.

It simply said that the show would consist of a band segment followed by a political interview segment followed by a closing band segment.

Clearly, a political dimension to the entertainment formula existed right from the get-go. Then I passed around another handout, my current minute-by-minute detailed show plan.

*See, it's different!* Major Hochstetter bellowed.

*How so? I countered.*

*It is not the same.*

I explained that "not the same" meant that I had broken the show up into more "digestible" bites. Instead of long band segments, I now offered multiple, short band segments. And between band segments – while the stage crew would make equipment adjustments – the radio host and I would interview a politician.

This way I could keep the show moving seamlessly. Overall, the same proportions of band time versus politician time remained intact. I had just reshuffled it to make a better show for the audience (see, it is entertainment-led).

*It's totally different*, The Major snorted, willfully disregarding the explanation.

"Are you really going with *this* as your fraud argument?" I wondered silently.

Thankfully, many in the room came to my rescue, asserting that his complaint held no basis.

Next, he let out a demand: *What does William Landers have to do with NEFest?*

*William Landers runs an Internet news station called Ameriborn.com. He knows most of the politicians in Connecticut, and he is my liaison to them, you know, to see who would be interested in being interviewed on stage during NEFest. What's wrong with that?*

*Are these all Republicans?* Hochstetter snarled.

*William, who by the way is a Constitutionalist, not a Republican, knows most of them, and all are invited. It will make NEFest interesting for everyone.*

Still determined to win him over, I went on to describe the show a little more, pointing out that even the political bits were barely political. I included them merely to provide an opportunity for the audience to see these political types in a different light.

And to reinforce my good intentions, I explained that my choice of Mike Huckabee as the headliner continued along the same lines. No one considers Mike a polarizing figure; everyone likes him.

Upon saying this, my friend, the Gestapo Major, blasted me again, *WELL I DON'T LIKE HIM!*, vehemently disagreeing with my last statement. Then he displayed his true colors, emotionally describing himself to the whole room as "very left wing."

I sensed the room finally breathe a collective sigh of relief with that admission out in the open. In that moment of Glasnost, he probably would have admitted that he hated Christmas had I pressed him.

I clarified my statement, acknowledging that perhaps Major Hochstetter might not admire Mr. Huckabee, but that every Republican, Independent, and Democrat who I had polled in trying to determine who would draw the biggest crowd – *every one of them* – liked Huckabee. I then turned to the Democratic Town Committee chief and reported that my findings did not bode well for him in 2012.

Finally, I got everyone to agree, even The Major, that Governor Huckabee is a gentleman and not a person who views the world with hate or anger in his heart.

Then it started up again. This time I could not use language such as "God" or "Traditional Family" in a municipally owned venue. I cringed. But almost everyone on the committee came to the 1st Amendment's rescue and refused to let this type of affront to America continue.

Next The Major launched the "This is a danger to the town" attack line. He acknowledged the sale of tickets would accurately indicate how many people would attend the show, which, in turn, formulated a metric for arranging adequate police coverage…

But, he said, such a calculation ignored *The Huckabee Factor.*

*With a personality such as Huckabee,* The Major postulated, *some 40,000 angry, ticketless* (I thought for a moment he said "shirtless"*) Tea-Party types would descend upon the town, ruining everything.*

Discussion ensued, cooler heads prevailed, and we eventually concluded that "Huckabee types" would not crash the gates.

Finally, my angry antagonist tried a procedural gimmick, asking the committee to re-vote on my proposal.

Had they re-voted, it would have sent the message that the show had fundamentally changed, and that I had fraudulently misled the town.

I pointed out these implications, and forcefully said that I would do all within my power not to let this type of intellectual dishonesty succeed. To its credit, the committee, comprising intelligent folk, - half Democrat and half Republican - quickly came to a consensus: No – there would be no second vote.

The meeting ended. Everyone emptied out into the parking lot, and the Democrat clan huddled on the far side for "the meeting *after* the meeting," and I guessed it probably had nothing to do with the Red Sox's standing in the American League.

*Below: The band at a 2010 TV appearance*

# Summer 2010 —
# The Hartford Symphony

The next morning, I meet with two CPAs. We discussed procedures for paying expenses and collecting revenues, and reviewed the legal and tax aspects of the company that I created to run the show. During this meeting, the ring of my cell phone interrupted us. Glancing at the display, I recognized the phone number of The Head of the Hartford Symphony Orchestra - HSO.

She asked if this were a good time to talk. I replied that I would wrap up my planning meeting and return her call in an hour.

Forty-five minutes later the accounting people said good-bye, and I planned to get a fresh coffee and return the call to the Symphony head, keen to make her acquaintance. As the accounting people started to leave, the phone rang again: It was her, the HSO Head. I rushed the accountants off and answered the phone with a pleasant "hello."

My caller came right to the point, in a highly agitated, autocratic tone of voice, insisting that the Symphony would no longer allow me to use its box office to sell the NEFest tickets.

She accused me of violating our contract, saying that the Symphony simply could not affiliate with right-wing organizations that use such language as "God and America" in their promotional materials. Doing so, she said, would jeopardize the Symphony's ability to secure government grant money... and then she muttered something about a pending bond issuance.

*As a politically unaffiliated, non-profit organization, the Symphony must remain unattached and untainted,* she said, *and so you must find another ticket vendor. Besides, the trustees want this whole thing to "just go away."*

I kept trying to interrupt her, but she kept right on talking…until she ran out of things to say. And at that point I asked, *Can I talk now or are we to hang up?*

Her silence granted me permission to speak, so I began.

*First*, I pointed out, *we are not affiliated. Your box office is just selling tickets on commission.*

*Second, this 'God and America' stuff… it's simply the title of my CD, nothing more, merely an intellectual proposition contemplating the evolving relationship between God and America.*

I told her that I graduated from Hartford's Trinity College, where a few professors recently completed an in-depth study on this drifting relationship. *Why on Earth could this create a problem?*

Third, I wanted to know how I had violated the contract.

She jumped back in with an assertion: *You were not to connect yourself to the Symphony in any way.*

Quoting the half-page contract in my folder, I pointed out the only "connection" existed as a couple of sentences stating The Symphony would receive $4 dollars per ticket, nothing more, and that she was interrupting my business based on pressure from her trustees, and without first checking the facts.

She said the decision to stop selling tickets was final.

I said the next voice she would hear on the matter would be a lawyer's, and I hung up.

I called my lawyer.

My lawyer called the Symphony.

My lawyer called me back.

*They will keep selling your tickets but they <u>ask</u> that you remove mention of the Symphony from your NEFest Web Site.*

*Where do we mention the Symphony?* I pondered.

Then I got it. When it comes time to buy tickets, they want my web page to say, "Click here to buy tickets" rather than "Click here for the Symphony box office." But, I pointed out to my lawyer, that once they click "Click here to buy tickets" the customer will connect to the Symphony site anyway, which then displays NEFest as an event one can select.

*They're fine with that*, my lawyer replied. *They just don't want you to mention the Symphony on your site.* At this point I thought of William Holden's line in "The Bridge Over The River Kwai": "Madness, madness."

But in an effort for peace I called my web designer and he changed it as I described.

I moved on. Late afternoon became early evening, and the members of my band, LittleHouse, arrived one by one for our rehearsal. Time to take off my promoter hat and replace it with my performer hat.

That night LittleHouse sounded great: tight, lots of energy, movement, and polish. We stood ready to play at NEFest along with the other exciting regional bands that would also appear.

The bands that I had invited to perform in the show knew each other pretty well. We all remained long-term Connecticut artists dedicated to our craft. Some had played in bands together in previous decades. All were accomplished veterans with original material and signature sounds. All had new CDs out in 2010.

I was pumped. Besides performing with my own band I would also perform in what I termed "The Bob Hope Role." This way, when I introduced an artist, I could give the audience the lowdown on them, facts such as "...this man earned 11 Grammy awards..." and "...this woman sang for years on a famous late night network show..." and so on.

The next day I went in to Town Hall to see the Mayor to get all of this ridiculous battling ended. After all, it was the Mayor and me who had signed the contract for use of the Simsbury Meadows facility; we were the principals, not the Democrat Party or The Hartford Symphony.

Plus, years before, during her first term, the Mayor had corrected a wrong that came my way, and I believed that she would stand up for any citizen as her top priority; I trusted that she had the discipline not to politicize things.

Boy, was I wrong. She might have been a straight shooter when she started in politics, but time and ambition must have turned her into a political creature.

We went to her office and had coffee, just like we had years ago during the first interaction already mentioned.

She started by saying that she had nothing to do with the meetings I was involved with, that her only thoughts were to run the town, and that she worked tirelessly toward that end. She pointed out that she wanted as little trouble as possible in doing so, and that she would never cause unnecessary conflict, but more to the point, that she did not control all of the others.

*But Mary, I protested, the Democratic Town Committee Chairman presided at my tribunal, and you are the top Democrat around here.*

*Plus, there was a lawyer there, who apparently is a personal friend of yours, who accused me of fraud concerning our contract, and aren't you a Trustee of the Hartford Symphony, the ones who tried to pull the plug on my ticket sales?*

*I don't control these people. I just want to run the town.*

We went on to talk about Huckabee.

*Mary, your problem is not Huckabee, it's Dan Malloy.*

Mary, at that moment, was running once again - though she had promised Simsbury that she would not run - for Lieutenant Governor in the Democratic primary with Ned Lamont, who was running for Governor.

Ned Lamont was the one who, a few years back, challenged Joe Lieberman for Connecticut's Senate seat (Joe was not left wing enough), causing Lieberman to go Independent (Joe L, a beloved state son, who ran for V.P. with Gore, won in a land side over Lemont, the rich socialist). Despite this blowout defeat, Ned Lamont was back again! At the moment the Lamont/Mary ticket was ahead in the polls against Dan Malloy and his running mate Nancy Wyman.

I told Mary that we had met Malloy, and that he will probably do the NEFest event. *From what I see, he has ice water in his veins. Malloy is your problem, not me, not Huck, not nobody.*

I added that she should definitely be on that stage.

*I don't care about the election. I only care about running Simsbury.*

I left.

*Live at the Warner Theater 2010 – Quite a line up!*

# Strange Days Have Found Us

The next morning I headed over to The Simsbury Performing Arts Center for a meeting to plan for the show: perimeter marshalling, ticket collection, and "will call" processing, as we anticipated more than 1,000 will call distributions (for the supporters of the politicians).

When I arrived, the sun bore down at 96 degrees with heavy humidity, so the site manager, the staff coordinator, the town's representative, and I moved into the air-conditioned trailers situated at the back of the stage and we began our meeting. We reviewed myriad details about parking, police, medical aid, and other logistical concerns.

Then the door opened and two senior gentlemen came in and sat down.

They introduced themselves as trustees of the Symphony. I did not object, even though they had invited themselves to my meeting. They certainly didn't own the Performance Center, although they acted as though they did. I had to remind myself that I didn't have a site license agreement with them; I had one with the Town of Simsbury.

But I figured, so what. Let them sit through this practical stuff and they'll see that all I am doing is putting on a show.

So we resumed our meeting again and got into the swamp of details. The trustees' demeanor, however, told me that they had no interest in these details. They just couldn't stand the fact that NEFest was happening, period.

Finally, one of them broke in to ask me about "God and America."

*It's political, right?*

I didn't mind. I repeated what I had told their executive a few days before about the intellectual nature of the statement. I reiterated the bit about the Trinity professors, and how the term would simply serve as the title of my upcoming CD release.

I wanted to go further to make the following points, but was interrupted before I could:

*Separation of church and state does not equate to the separation of God and America. Churches and states are organized institutions, and our constitution does not want these institutions to mess with each other. 'Church and State,' is about the protocol between institutions, get it?*

*Now God, in whatever form you choose, is not an institution. And neither is America. America is the entire entity, the whole thing, an organic human/ geographical biosphere. It includes our history, our traditions, the land, the amber waves of grain and the spacious skies – and it also happens to house a bunch of institutions like churches and governmental entities.*

*So stop applying separation of church and state beyond its domain. Benjamin Franklin, not a big churchgoer, coined it best with: "In God We Trust." So I think that 'God and America' is a fine bit of language, and I just wish you guys from the Symphony would stop showing up at my meetings…*

But I did not bring this church and state stuff up, because before I could do so, the other trustee confronted me. This guy cited the term "Traditional American Families" as contained in my advertising.

I asked the trustee to come to his point. He looked at me and whispered, *You know, it's racial, right?*

*Racial,* I asked, *where do you get racial?*

*'Traditional' – you know, as in 'blacks can't marry whites.'*

At this point I no longer wanted to win these guys over. I told them that Traditional American Families are ones that like the America they grew up with – and who basically want to keep it that way. *LET ME SPELL IT OUT*, I insisted…

*T R A D I T I O N A L – WE LIKE OUR TRADITIONS*
*A M E R I C A N – WE LIKE AMERICA.*
*F A M I L I E S – WE LIKE OUR FAMILIES*

*And look, I know you wanna know, so I might as well tell you guys about where I stand politically …*

As the words left my mouth, I thought but didn't say:

*"Or else you will keep coming to my meetings, inadvertently affiliating yourselves and your left-wing Symphony organization with mine. And I don't want to be affiliated with you.*

*You guys are the perfect Stalinists. Muzzle the enemy at all costs.*

So all I said about my politics was:

*… I don't want to change America. Beside Britain, Canada, and Australia, we are the only country that goes for personal self-reliance and liberty. It took thousands of years for this type of freedom to evolve and I don't want to mess it up.*

*That's my politics.*

The meeting ended, and I walked out into the burning sun.

I Googled the long-range weather forecast. I saw that my show date would prove as brutally hot as this day. I also thought about those Symphony trustees, their executive, and their friends on the Democrat Town Committee, plus Mary the Mayor, the Symphony trustee.

I couldn't believe the Symphony had the audacity to claim that I tainted their "politically unaffiliated" status. They didn't need affiliation to be tainted. They exist as a self-tainted political organization in their own right. Taxpayer-financed grant money for them … no way, if you ask me.

I left the Performance Center and drove to a popular talk radio host's house - the one who I hoped would do the interviewing. I told him what was what, and he convinced me to pull the plug, keep my powder dry, and live to fight another day.

He said that the worst would be unleashed over the remaining two weeks until I would be beaten down, operating in embattled chaos. Then I would lose my shirt.

He proved, as always, convincing.

I drove home to unravel the event.

And just think, the Left operates in this "Silence them" manner today in every micro-facet of our society. My use of the term "Stalinists"?

Hardly an exaggeration.

# Fall 2010 —
# Welcome to The Barn

*Above: live in the barn*

Ever since the demise of NEFest in July of 2010 it seemed that I constantly appeared in the crosshairs of local Simsbury Democrat extremists. After trying to bring Huckabee (a danger to us all) to town, I guess I was marked.

My trouble with Democrat operatives during NEFest, demonstrates just how dedicated these political bees can be in stinging to the death anyone not from the hive. Just to reiterate, I did not go looking for them; I simply pursued my music/politics show thing, and they swarmed after me *en masse*.

In contrast, never once have I raised a hand against liberals to end their freedom of expression. All I have ever done is argue with them. Of course, until now, when I decided to write about them and their socialist wiring.

In August, when I returned from a family trip to Russia, people said that in my absence a Tea Party protest took place at town hall, and the word on the street had it that I arranged it – from Russia! Nonsense.

I ignored this stuff, seeking only to get my band playing in front of people again, and so I started up the "Welcome To The Barn" shows again in September of 2010 in the barn on my private property. Over the summer I had written a dozen new songs, and a friend-and-family event in my barn would accurately gauge each song's appeal.

These free "Welcome To The Barn" shows, as we call them, proved charming and intimate, with guests sitting on couches and benches to absorb the performance.

Well guess what? When I started the barn shows up again, they came back -- the attack bees, that is. I was so naive. You see, once I had canceled NEFest, which meant that I canceled the dreaded Huckabee, I figured that the bees would no longer swarm. After all, the dreaded Huckabee would no longer venture into Connecticut. He would stay down in NYC, taping his FOX shows.

So I figured that would make the bees happy. But no, the guy who tried to bring Huck to Connecticut (that would be me) was still alive, and so not only were ninja attack bees back, but this time the hive had reinforcements: actual Town of Simsbury employees. These employees survive under the thumb of their boss, the Mayor, a Queen Bee and very ambitious lefty, who, as noted, twice ran for a deputy governor's seat - once removed from the Governor's office.

In September of 2010, I started getting a whole lot of local press coverage due to the buzz already created by the recently canceled NEFest show. Suddenly, LittleHouse appeared on local NBC, CBS, ABC and FOX TV shows, in a bunch of local papers, plus in the state's paper of record, *The Hartford Courant*, and, finally, in *The New York Times*.

All-in-all, pretty good exposure for Littlehouse, except that in one of the town papers, the article said we were charging $25 per ticket for the local barn shows: not true. The barn shows were free. The $25 idea applied to our theatre aspirations. I had planned to rent theaters, like Beanie suggested – and eventually did so -, with the hope that people would pay $25 to see us. But at the barn we never charged a penny in admission.

You see, if I were to charge for tickets, then it would be a business (a commercial category), which would mean that the town could regulate it for safety and a myriad of other reasons.

But I never did charge money. Still by sticking with the erroneous mantra that I had charged money, the Mayor and her operatives sought to create a so-called "land use issue" that did not actually exist. This way they could swarm in and demand that the town send the Fire Marshall and the Building Inspector in to find something.

How dare *LittleHouse* do this American singing stuff at home on private property in front of family and friends!

I got wind of the coming assault when a straight-shooter from Zoning called me, saying that "gadflies" had descended on the town, citing the running-a-business angle as reason to unleash the might of the Town against me. This town employee said he called me to check the facts. I told him the details.

He said he had heard from others that I didn't charge to get into shows, but he wanted to know for sure. I told him that it was a misprint and that we had already asked the newspaper that any monetary reference to <u>barn</u> tickets be removed going forward. And besides, as we both agreed, the barn shows were so small, that making a business out of them did not make sense anyway.

Facts made clear, case closed. Or so I thought.

# There's Something About Mary

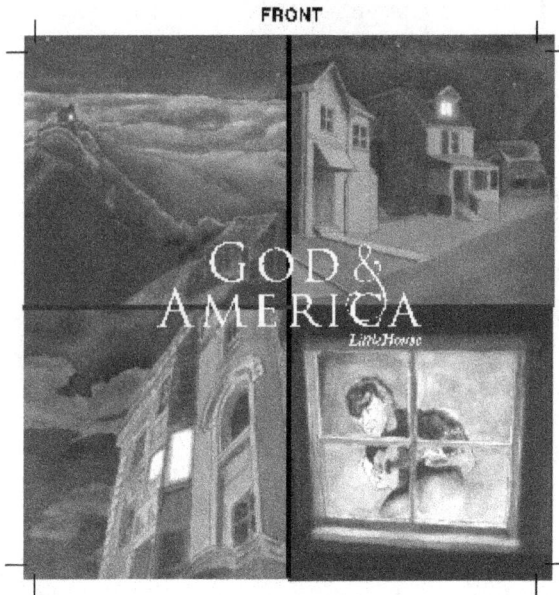

*The 2010 God & America CD*

Time went by. *LittleHouse* had a few more smashing barn shows (they really were quite well received), and then one day a notice arrived via registered mail from The Town of Simsbury. Looking concerned, and without saying a word, my wife placed a registered mail notice slip on the breakfast table in front of me.

Later that morning, on the way to the recording studio where I worked on the band's material each day, I stopped at the local post office to fetch this registered letter. I was pretty sure of what it contained. I opened it and removed a letter from The Zoning Guy, the very person with whom I had such a lucid talk with two weeks prior. From the looks of it, though, someone else told him what to write and he just had to sign it.

The first two paragraphs of the letter acknowledged that the barn shows took place on private property and that we did not charge admission. Hence with those two facts established, the town acknowledged that my hoedowns constituted private functions, not under the authority of the town.

But a cryptic third paragraph claimed that the barn shows appeared so unusual in it's "traffic" (this is a commercial term; it did not mean cars), that The Town must (somehow) have the authority to enter the property. It looked as if someone in town hall stood determined to manufacture a basis to bloody me once and for all for the Huckabee stuff.

The paragraph was gobbledygook, but it did contain the tone of authority. Written by a professional, maybe the town attorney, maybe by Major Hochstetter or the like.

Its purpose was to scare me into letting them onto the property, even though no legal case had been put forward.

I stuck the letter in my pocket, and continued onto the recording studio to work on my songs, as mentioned, a daily practice.

A few days later, the Tuesday before Thanksgiving in 2010, while again at the recording studio, I took a call from a man who told me his name, as if I should know him, but did not identify his position (later I would learn he was the Building Inspector). This stranger wanted to set a time for himself and the Fire Marshall to come over and inspect the barn.

I said "No" about 10 times, saying that just because whoever he worked for threw the word "traffic" around in a letter, that they had not presented clear legal authority or purpose to justify coming onto private property. I said I would get a lawyer and we hung up.

A little later that morning the Fire Marshall called. We chatted, and he politely listened to all of my "principles" regarding private property in America … and so, to reciprocate for his patient tone and his promise to present legal authority, I agreed to meet him down at the main firehouse (the town has five branch firehouses as well, which is unbelievable). We set the meeting for the Monday morning after Thanksgiving, six days hence.

I immediately phoned the Mayor, someone, as you know, I knew. I left a message, and around noon she returned my call. I mentioned the letter I had received from the town, my talk with both The Building Inspector (I found this out from the Marshall) and the Fire Marshall, and Mary said to come over at 3:30 that afternoon to discuss it.

When I arrived, the Mayor had the Town Planner with her, who supervised The Zoning Officer, the man who had sent me the letter, who is different from the building guy, who called me to fix a meeting with the fire guy.

We first covered the fact that I did not charge any admission. Still, Mary insisted that I had "triggered" the whole thing by the paper saying that I did charge money, and now she found herself in the middle, owing answers to the good citizens complaining (about what she didn't say).

I pointed out that inaccurate information in the newspaper, once straightened out, meant "case closed," and that the town should tell all of the gadflies that it reviewed the situation, that monies are not being charged, and that my barn remains just a private residence event, outside of town jurisdiction.

Then I asked her to read the cryptic third paragraph. My point: someone in <u>her</u> administration would not to let this die.

*Mary, this letter has a lawyer's fingerprints all over it. Your zoning guy did not write it.*

The letter's attempt to argue jurisdiction - a twisted, hard-to-follow, manufactured jurisdiction - based upon the word "traffic," simply smelled political.

I said that it was not right for a political agenda to be in play. The Mayor said she was not party to anything like that. Again, her whole purpose was to run the town smoothly, not to create trouble.

I reminded her this was what she told me during the summer when I met with her about NEFest. Even if - somehow - she kept her hands clean of this obvious politicizing of town authority, she was, after all, the local head of the Democrats, and perhaps more – having just run for lieutenant governor – again.

The meeting ended by her agreeing to look into things a little deeper. Mary said that either she or the planning manager would get back to me. They never did, so I assumed they had dropped it.

The simple fact was that I had come to her as my Mayor in good faith for help, and she decided to ignore her duty to uphold the rule of law.

As I got ready to leave, Mary looked away and said *"The Fire Marshall is another matter; I don't control him."*

Fine, I thought, Mary is like a kleptomaniac, who believes she cannot be caught. She has lost her moral compass and is going to let the fire guy take the heat (pun fully intended), thinking I wouldn't figure it out.

Over the Thanksgiving break, I spoke to many folks around town about these developments in Simsbury, and the impact they had upon me. I wanted their honest impressions, and so I made sure that I described matters plainly without making the Mayor, the town officials, or the Fire Marshall out to be bad guys.

Each time I brought the topic up in this neutral manner, my conversation partners would go into "lifesaver mode," telling me that the Fire Marshall was a notorious bully who would trick me, and who would never let up once he had his hooks into me. Didn't I know all this? What planet did I call home?

I said that I did not know all of this, that I had spent the last 30 years on the East Side of Manhattan where this stuff is not part of New York's purpose (read: making money). Plus, I was a bit of a Libertarian, minding my own business, and not following the dramas playing out in town.

Every disinterested person I spoke with, though, had his or her own Fire Marshall "nightmare" story, plus they warned me about the Mayor, the puppet master pulling all of the strings, sending out her "No See 'ems" to do her bidding.

"She uses legal minutia to throw up obstacles and deludes people in such a way that no one can catch her."

Ouch!

But most of all, they wanted to shake me out of my naiveté, telling me about the demands the fire department had placed on them, and how the fire department had the town, including the mayor, in a financial headlock, automatically getting tax money without people getting to vote for or against it, and then using this money to build all of these expensive firehouses around town, stocked with trucks and equipment, that pretty much sat and did nothing.

Just as nature abhors a vacuum, Simsbury's "volunteer" Fire Department had maneuvered itself over the years to glean so much money and power that it just had to be used.

Could things in my hometown be this outrageous? Well, after a bunch of these conversations I started to get it. We were in a Star Trek episode where the Mayor and fire department ran the government like rival mafia bosses! Kirk, Spock, McCoy ... where the heck are you?

# Thanksgiving 2010 —
# The Fire Marshall

The Fire Marshall had graduated after me at Simsbury High School. In my 30-year absence from Simsbury while making my way in the world and living in NYC, The Marshall, like most people, stayed put in Simsbury, fine by me. At some point he became king of the hill in the fire department. Again, fine, someone has to do it.

I wanted to meet with him now that I heard so much about him, plus I wanted to see the new "Main" Firehouse recently built on Simsbury's Main Street, the building many called "The Taj Mahal." Of course the real Taj Mahal was built for an Indian Prince's wife. The Marshall, they said, built our Taj Mahal, for, as you have already guessed, The Marshall. It was apparently a love match made in heaven.

Walking into the Main Firehouse's fabulous glass lobby I saw two huge six-foot photos of the two most-famous fires in Simsbury's history, both about 45 years ago. I had witnessed both fires during my teenage years, somewhere in the 1960s (a blur).

One photo portrayed The First Church of Christ Fire, a church built, more or less, by the Pilgrims. An electrical fire caused by trees falling onto power lines, as I recall, the fire was partially contained, saving the main church's walls, but the roof and everything under it disappeared. Talk around town blamed lack of water from the fire trucks. I went to look with my father the next day watching a crane dismantle what remained of the burnt-out steeple. It took years to rebuild the church.

The second huge photo depicted was The Great Hoskins Road Tobacco Barn Fire. One tobacco barn caught fire, which led to the next one catching fire, and so on, like dominoes. About six went down. No one could do anything.

Each barn had a propane tank that fed open metal heaters used to cure the tobacco hanging in its rafters. As each barn caught fire, its propane tank would blow, causing an enormous explosion that echoed down the valley.

I lived across from this tobacco farm – Farm #1 – and saw the flames through the woods while playing wiffle ball in my back yard. The barns burned for hours. We saw everything; nothing was saved. The poor distraught manager of Farm #1, a man I once worked for as a tobacco picker, kept running into the burning barns attempting to save the crop, only to be dragged out by the fire fighters and then consoled by his wife and children. You might find this interesting: Martin Luther King Jr. worked Farm #1 in the 1940's.

The three dilapidated barns still standing on Hoskins Road today survived because the wind blew the fire away from them, down the line in the opposite direction.

I guess you get my point about the fires, but I'll spell it out anyway. These fires occurred 45 years ago. They proved the biggest fires in the town's history, and no one could put them out. You can't put fires out once they get going. So what's with the six firehouses filled with $250,000 trucks (they probably cost even more, but so what?), and all the bullying?

After admiring the gigantic photos, I looked to my right and there stood the wife of my childhood best friend. She had worked as the dispatcher for the Simsbury fire department for three decades.

We said our hellos, but not much else, as she knew I was there on official business, so she brought me to The Marshall's office.

Accompanying me that day was the fellow who worked on my barn when we fixed it up to be a band performance space. Before doing the work - hanging theater lights, putting in a heating/air-conditioning unit and installing insulation and thermal windows and doors – this fellow and many other construction guys had checked out the barn for structural soundness, verifying that the barn's studs and beams stood strong in all in the right places and in the right proportions.

I consider safety paramount – who wouldn't - and I brought this master craftsman to the Taj Mahal with me so that we could describe the barn to The Fire Marshall.

The Marshall took us to a new state-of-the-art conference room. This was no fire station, but a corporate headquarters with granite counters, leather chairs, and artwork. He brought a pile of statute and fire codebooks with him. I couldn't wait, really.

I recapped some of the "private property is sacred" stuff that we had already discussed on the phone a week earlier, but then told him about the people I had met since that phone call who had all warned me about him.

This did not bother him in the least. The more upset the citizenry then the better he must be doing in his safety job. No matter the criticism, the Marshall was there to provide for the very safety of the town. People just did not get it. Zero tolerance and all that, but to me, he represented the head of a Fahrenheit 451 squad (a movie from the 1960s where the fire department burns books and non-desirables down).

Safety. Safety is sacred. Safety above all (even the Constitution), we must all be for safety. What a bit!

Next he opened all of the legal books to explain to me why he held the authority to inspect my private property. He had dropped the "traffic" angle, and he now based his authority upon a statute (which he did not show me) wherein if there were "Public Assembly" of over 49 people, that he had jurisdiction - even on a private residence, and even with no charging of an admission fee. This Public Assembly statute, he pointed out, allowed him to examine churches, for example, as churches stood open to the public and they invited free assembly.

I take over … in protest!

*But my situation is the very opposite of "Public Assembly". My shows are not open to the public. They are by invitation only; your name must appear on the guest list. And we certainly do not invite "assembly"; I have a security guard at the end of the driveway to prevent free assembly.*

*Well we're "going with" Public Assembly*, he asserted.

*Going with? Can you make me copies of the statutes that pertain to me*, I asked?

*No*, he replied. *That would be a violation of copyright laws* (which of course is not true, according to my lawyer friends).

His attempt to bamboozle me with a copyright dodge regarding government publications actually shocked me, but I stayed quiet about it and moved on. I had been warned (about him).

Ok, I proposed, *say you do get a court order to get into the barn. What fire codes would we be looking at that pertain to my situation?*

He replied that he could not say without seeing the barn firsthand.

*Ok, how about if I draw you a footprint of the barn?*

Of course, I added, that I realized that a drawing would not be an official inspection or anything like that, but it would allow us to see the codes to which I would be exposed.

I drew a sketch of the barn's 30-by-40-foot floor plan on a sheet of paper, showing the three exit doors, the bench/couch layout, and the band performance area.

This got him started. He began reading the code...

*Sprinklers ... no, you don't need sprinklers...*

*Exit Lights ... no, you don't need exit lights, there are no staircases or hallways...*

*Fire Extinguishers ... no, you don't need them.*

*Ah ha! But I have these anyway* I exclaimed with glee.

*Ok*, he said, *but maybe your three exit doors are too close together. If there were a fire – say, in between them - then people would be trapped.*

Pointing to my sketch I said that *it would have to be a terrorist attack – by the Taliban - on this very wall for that to happen, but yes, it could happen ... Now I understand your concern* (a similar expression to 'I feel your pain'). I continue ...

*But that is just a theoretical danger. Doesn't there need to be a clear and present danger to justify your getting involved?*

I thought I had won him over with sheer reasonableness. Please note, that the Fourth Amendment in the Bill of Rights strictly prohibits <u>unreasonable</u> search and seizure. There must be a clear and present danger. But as my liberal friends point out, the Constitution merely serves as a guideline.

The meeting suddenly ended with him giving me three hours to get back to him or else … he would go to a judge for a court order.

I took this act of intimidation calmly. I had hoped that he would have said something like … I'll think about it and give you a call if I want you to do anything.

But I guess old habits die hard, and so I got the same treatment that, over the decades, hundreds, if not thousands of citizens have received from The Fire Marshall of Simsbury.

A month went by. I heard nothing… so much for 5 PM.

Then, a week before Christmas, another registered mail slip arrived from the Building Inspector, this one addressed to my wife Laura, in whose name the property is held. Aha, they're going for the soft underbelly. Don't these guys know that she practices Karate?

Since the slip bore Laura's name, she immediately drove to the post office and redeemed it for a mean, nasty letter (with circles and arrows) from the Building Inspector. The letter went on to say that because we never made contact with the Fire Marshall - after they sent the *first* mean and nasty letter (from before Thanksgiving, as sent by Zoning) - that this neglect on <u>our</u> part left them no choice but to pursue legal action against us, including potential fines and arrest.

The Building Inspector, in his letter, also made it clear that like The Fire Marshal, he, too, was a state guy, and not beholden to the local town government. This way, no one in town (other than the Mayor who could fire him) could corrupt him.

I read this with relief. And I could hear Mayor Mary saying, "See, I don't control these people," even though it is her duty to do so under the town's charter.

No, his bible was the state building code manual, which apparently sits above Mayor Mary and the U.S. Constitution.

My wife's knees buckled, as Karate did not train its students for the potential of arrest by a state official. But I told her not to panic, that George Washington had it a lot worse when he stood up to the entire British Empire without a budget (or real teeth). And, as we all know, it worked out OK for George, except for the wooden teeth part, as federal employees at that time did not get dental care benefits, and so, "In God We Trust," it would all work out for us, too.

With that, Laura, my wife, took a deep breath and became A FREEDOM FIGHTER.

Well anyway, with all kidding aside - and in contrast of our little world compared to Washington's – our trouble centered on the town's Building Inspector, the author of the latest letter, and whoever was pushing him, not the entire British Empire.

Of course one must recognize that his letter spoke on behalf of the Mayor, the Fire Marshall (who, we have learned, is also part of the state government's untouchable squad) and ultimately, on behalf of the entire frightened American people desperately seeking building and fire safety in their private homes.

So, not having a clue at what to do with this government encroachment stuff - something to which at 58 years of age I had never been acclimated - and not inclined to hire a lawyer, I wrote the building inspector a "common sense" response letter, pointing out that I had done everything possible to communicate with the town, and that still the town had yet to present me with a legal framework authorizing an inspection. Being a communicative person - one who ensures that communication has been accomplished - I went down to town hall on December 22$^{rd}$ to hand-deliver my letter to the Mayor and to the Building Inspector.

I walk up to Mary's office, and there she stands. Mary, a lawyer, tries not to appear too bright, so that you think she is a sweetheart. Still, not able to hold back, and seeing the letter in my hand, she says "Is that a love letter for me?"

Yes, I replied.

Then she reminded me that this whole mess resulted from my appearances on TV and in the papers and that she was only doing her duty and had to follow up when citizens complained. *You brought this whole thing upon yourself.*

Never mind that months ago, she and I had already covered the $25-per-ticket misprint thing in the newspaper, and that she had promised to look into it and by now she should be telling the worried citizens that it was just a misprint, and so, it is a private property matter after all, not under the town's jurisdiction and … well, case closed.

Mary - the lawyer – looked at me as if my logic did not register with her. I knew right then and there that she was into it – politically – in earnest. I just couldn't fathom why.

I thought of a quote from Sam Adams: *How strangely will the Tools of a Tyrant pervert the plain Meaning of Words.*

Finally, I showed her the sentence in my letter asking for information about my case, based upon the *Connecticut Freedom Of Information Act.* She brushed it off. *No problem.* Months later, when I requested such information again, her assistant actually wrote me saying that the town bore no obligation to respond as my request for the few town documents about me appeared too broad.

Anyway, after speaking to Mary about love letters, I walked across the hall to Town Planning.

I met The Building Inspector - for the first time, by the way, and I like him - but then he started to say a few words about concerns for the public's safety at the barn. I realized then that my letter, with all of its points, was not to be read by anyone. Nevertheless, I asked him to please read the letter and, believe it or not, I asked him to speak to the town lawyer about it so that we might get a little help in moving the situation along based upon <u>the actual rule of law.</u>

*Below: The 2010 Old School CD*

OLD SCHOOL
*LittleHouse*

# Winter 2011 —
# The Invasion of Private Property

A week later, somewhere around New Year's Eve, my wife informed me that we received another warning letter from my new pen pal at the building department. Go figure!

By then, I had scheduled a deep winter "Welcome to The Barn" Littlehouse show in January. As always, there was no charge and only pre-approved guests were to allowed into the Barn. My wife performed her habitual role of maintaining the guest list for the security guard (who prevented public assembly). Sensing imminent government aggression, I nevertheless kept my cool; after all, this was still America (for now), and not Russia (which I had just visited in August) – I just needed to stand my ground. I waited.

Later that week, at 10:00 one morning, I sat at my bedroom computer, sifting through my emails when my wife walked in with a familiar, funny expression and said, *There's a guy waiving a badge at the door.*

That funny expression serves my wife faithfully as an involuntary nonverbal message that she bears bad news. After 20 years of marriage I could read these signals like street signs, so without pressing for details, I quickly put on my shoes and raced through the house to the side foyer.

Standing not at the door but already inside my foyer appeared Detective X. I had met him previously when local kids stole my utility golf cart. I liked Detective X, an Iraq veteran and a positive fellow. Still, he should not have stepped into my house, as the warrant he would present concerned only the barn.

He handed me the warrant, even though my wife owned the house and had not appointed me as her legal representative.

Also already in the foyer was the Building Inspector, one of the guys who would conduct the inspection. They did not explain the objective of their visit.

Outside I saw a town "black and white" with a uniformed officer in the role of police backup. Then I saw The Zoning Inspector – the stand-up guy – eyes cast down, as if ashamed, and, next, The Fire Marshall, pacing by the barn doors… and my blood began to boil at this parade of force and intimidation.

I started ranting at my building inspector friend, who, as I noted, I actually liked to some degree, but certainly not when standing uninvited in my foyer.

*"You did it. You actually did it. You went to a judge, bamboozled him into thinking this was a Commercial, Public Assembly situation, and now you are breaking the law, forcing yourself onto my property with an ill-gotten search and seizure warrant. You should leave now before you go any further with this lunacy!"*

He just smiled.

And so, after warning him to back off, and quickly realizing he would not respect my rights, I stepped past him and went outside, passing the uniformed cop. *What are you looking at?* I roared at him.

*Don't worry about us* he replied, *we're just here to watch.* I felt better, thinking that, maybe, the police chief hated this un-American, illegal role forced upon them. But still, he occupied my property, illegally!

I walked 10 steps further to confront The Fire Marshall, who I had already confronted months earlier, saying again that he had no business trying to inspect an invitation-only, free-admission, songwriting workshop held on private property. I accused him of breaking the law as well.

Then I calmed down and unlocked the barn. They had the guns, and I did not know how they would proceed. If they trampled my rights, I would get to that another time. For now, I wanted to avoid immediate and unpredictable measures by authority figures bearing loaded weapons – such as perhaps ending up with the side of my face against a police cruiser hood, wearing a pair of handcuffs behind my back..

This excessive demonstration of force stripped me of options, as I am indeed old enough to remember Kent State.

The zoning guy did not enter the barn. I took further comfort in the fact that he couldn't even look me in the eye as I passed by him. But the building and fire guys stepped right in and got their first look.

*It's just as I described to you*, I protested to The Marshall. Then, dressed in his Fire Marshall outfit, he pulls out a Polaroid camera and starts snapping shots of the barn rafters.

*What on Earth are you filming, K….? What are you looking for?* By law they are required to tell you their mission – what they are there to search (examine) or seize.

The Marshall ignored me and continued to take his snap shots.

I suddenly knew how Arlo Guthrie felt when Officer Obie took the 27, 8"-by-10" glossy photos with circles and arrows and notations on the back about the Thanksgiving dinner garbage. Arlo was defenseless. Obie wore the guns.

The Building Inspector weighed in (literally), hopping up and down on the oak floor, noting the barn's substantial construction. I sensed that he felt glad to give me a pass, so that the Marshall could be the bad guy, instead of his boss, The Mayor. And sure enough, the Marshall took the bait and said something about the doors.

*What about the doors?* I queried.

*The code says you only need two* he began…

*But I have three*, I interrupted, *just like I drew for you in your office.*

*The code calls for them to be a certain distance apart based on the room's diagonal,* he continued, and he starts to measure the diagonal.

*You're gonna make me put in a forth door, aren't you?* I predicted.

*It's code,* he stated solemnly.

*If I put in a fourth door I will be 200 percent of code, in a tiny building with no corridors or steps, with three doors that empty right onto the driveway. What* *about the 4<sup>th</sup>* (Amendment of the U.S. Constitution) – <u>*Unreasonable*</u> *Search and Seizure? If this is reasonable, then the 4<sup>th</sup> just died.*

He put it this way: *If you have a show Saturday night and that fourth door is not installed and operational, I'll call the state police to shut you down and arrest you.*

*But you have no proper legal authority to be here in the first place. You just bamboozled a judge into giving you a bogus search warrant under "Public Assembly." Mary has tricked you into chasing a manufactured authority/no cause case. The 4<sup>th</sup> Amendment requires you to act on* <u>*specific knowledge of present danger*</u>*, and you are just making it all up.*

The next morning, Saturday, in five-degrees-above-zero weather, two friends of mine come over and install a door. The Fire Marshall comes by at 5 pm and gives us "permission" to do the show.

I told him that I would not let the matter rest, that his contempt for private property and the U.S. Constitution constituted a clear danger to society, and that I would have him and the other town employees, particularly Mayor Mary, held accountable for this illegal, excessive behavior.

He shrugged his shoulders and left.

*The main Firehouse*

# 2011 —
# The Ban on Charities

After the barn invasion incident of January 2011, I felt fairly dejected by what I had learned – the hard way – about my local government, but, as with the NEFest incident, I decided to move on.

I came up with a new idea. I would organize shows inside the barn and on other stages in support of various charities. This would enable me to meet new people and discover all of the nooks and crannies of the community as I experienced each charity's interests and ways.

From January 2011 onward *LittleHouse* hosted a bunch of these private events, and it worked out just as I had hoped.

But the Mayor stepped in yet again.

In June of 2011, almost a year after the canceled *NEFest show, LittleHouse* ended up performing a *Summer Solstice Show* at Simsbury Meadows – yes, on the town's stage. My concept for the charity aspect of the show worked like this: when someone bought a premium table for eight guests near the stage, they could elect to designate that table as either a Lupus Foundation or an Afghan Girls Fund table; the town would still keep the money, but *LittleHouse* would match it and contribute the matched amount to the respective charity.

Mary and her town attorney said no. If I were to perform on the town's stage, I was not to have any public affiliation with charities, for, in their reasoning, "It would not be fair to other charities."

These two lawyers presented this argument with a straight face! Moreover, they made me sign a contract wherein I agreed to limit my freedom of speech by not saying or printing anything dealing with religion or politics (this document remains in the town's possession; they refused to give me a copy).

I resented this temporary muzzling, but at least I knew from which sick corner they came. But for the life of me, I couldn't understand the ban on charity giving. But then I thought about it, and this seemingly "nutty" position against charitable giving ain't so nutty upon closer look.

Giving to charity means that you stand free (from the government) to help someone else, and it provides the receiver with a source of relief (other than the government). Charities thwart the goal of some government forces to steer people toward dependency on that same government.

The 2011 summer ban on supporting charities gave way to a new ban that autumn. This second anti-charity attack arose after *LittleHouse* hosted an event for a four-year old boy afflicted at birth by a terminal disease. His parents asked if I would do a barn show benefit. We held it in October of 2011.

One week later, another town letter from Zoning arrived saying that the town needed to reexamine the property – yes, a second time – for fire and building safety concerns, and demanded that I answer a slew of questions, providing my responses in writing.

I knew that zoning did not write this letter. Mind you, The Zoning Inspector was actually present when the first search and seizure masquerade went down the previous January, and so he certainly knew that everything about my barn already met the town's complete satisfaction – even though they had no right to demand such satisfaction.

I remained convinced that the letter originated in The Mayor's office.

Still, I went to see The Zoning Guy, as the letter appeared over his forced signature, and he admitted: *Yes, we know it was a fundraiser.*

*Then why don't you tell people it was a fundraiser so that they stop hassling me?*

*I guess it's just another case of 'no good deed goes unpunished,' and if you are fined, the town has already agreed to contribute the fine to the boy.*

This absurdity – fining me as a business and then giving the fine right back because the business is not a business but a charity, just so they could play cat-and-mouse with me - was the last of many straws that each reeked of out-of-control government stench. I said I would not acknowledge the letter, and that they could take whatever action they deemed appropriate in response.

Right after that, up here in the Northeast, we had a fluke snowstorm while all of the hardwood trees still held their leaves. Tens of thousands of trees came down and we all lost electric power for 10 days.

Our Mayor took to the airwaves and explained to the world the goodness of her government in giving 6,000 "free" (taxpayer paid) hot-cooked meals to Simsbury's citizens at the high school (a building paid for and maintained by taxpayer money) during the blackout.

That next week on November 4th the citizenry of Simsbury re-elected Mary by a 60-percent margin.

But it makes my point, "There shall only be but One Permissible Source of Charity, and it is through the Mercy of Your Government, the Mayor Locally.

Hey! What on Earth is going on?

When George Washington warned us of the single-mindedness of government to control, I never extrapolated it could deteriorate to this!

Anyway, when I told The Zoning Guy that I would not respond to the latest letter that he did not write, I also asked him to tell who actually wrote these letters… and he would not.

I realized that I would have to sue the town and get depositions to ever find out.

I huddled with a few lawyers about it and they figured it would cost me hundreds of thousand of dollars to bring an action against the government, though illegalities could possibly lead to criminal prosecution of the Mayor or the Fire Marshall, but that it would all be for naught, as I had suffered abstract damages (my well being), and that other than violations of my civil rights, which, unless you are poor, are hard to collect. I would squander my savings against the town's unlimited legal-defense budget – again, another taxpayer-funded resource – which in reality existed to protect Mary and any others implicated.

What a racket!

So, again, I left it alone, reluctantly and ruefully turning the other cheek.

Welcome to the Barn.

# Summer 2012 —
# The Circus Letter

I continued with the "Welcome To The Barn" workshops, and heard nothing else from the town until nine months later, during the summer of 2012, when I received "The Circus Letter."

Now, get this … The Circus Letter, again signed by the same Zoning officer, claimed that, under a Connecticut statute giving municipalities authority to regulate circuses in order to control dangerous animals, the town held new-found authority to investigate my barn…

My new lawyer called Zoning, and agreed for me to meet the Zoning official at Peaberry's, the local coffee shop.

At the cordial meeting, the Zoning officer acknowledged that I had no legal obligation to respond to the town in writing, but he proposed that I write a boiled-down letter explaining my "Welcome To The Barn" shows, and if I did, that he would get approval signatures attached to the letter from the police chief, the Fire Marshall, himself (Zoning), and the building inspector. These signatures would sanctify the use of my barn for the shows for one year.

I protested that my point remained constant: I did not need their approval, period, as my events constituted private functions on private property, with a security guard present to prevent public assembly. I did not want any part of this twisted stuff.

I sipped my coffee, contemplated, and eventually, agreed to write the letter for them to sign, as I realized that all of these departments might be angling for this distasteful saga to simply go away.

A signed letter by such a group of town luminaries would side-step M...
and her political minions from making these guys pursue me in violation their
actual departmental duties and the law itself. I would write the letter and see
where they'd take it.

*Below: a danger to us all – LittleHouse at Simsbury Meadows*

# Winter 2013 —
# Back To the Garden

So I wrote the letter explaining my music shows in August of 2012 and submitted it to The Zoning Guy.

Eventually the town's magistrates all signed it, but did so only six months later in February 2013. The strange coincidence of this delayed timing? The seemingly wayward letter arrived in my mailbox promptly after my mother ran into Mayor Mary (they know one other), and cautioned Mary to "stop picking" on me, saying *"Joe has the time and wherewithal to deal with the matter."*

So the promised letter finally surfaced. The Fire Marshall signed it, too, but penciled in a caveat to his approval, noting approved, but only "…as of the inspection date," in case I had since removed the fourth door or something.

Now, in April of 2013, as I complete the diary you read, this bizarre letter sits in my file.

My overall point boils down to the following: When a town's citizens have no idea that their mayor executes her power of office in the manner I have described herein, then she has effected, in stealth, a fundamental power shift against her own people … something that we generally refer to as "Abuse of Power."

At this point, three years into the madness, I implore you: We Must Return to The Garden - the one in which I grew up… but in doing so, we need New Gardeners – either Democrats or Republicans – so long as they are Americans –Who know how our Garden Grows.

*Below: The author, a "Traditional American"*

# Scope of Legal Issues

I am not an attorney, but my gut instinct remains that during these transgressions, at least several town officials broke both the spirit and letter of the law. I did not know, however, which laws came into play.

So I performed some research and categorized the laws in play into four types:

- Color of Law (abuse of power)
- The 4th Amendment (search & seizure)
- Freedom of Information
- Civil Rights

Let's extrapolate these …

# Color of Law Federal Statutes
# (AKA Abuse of Power)

---

*Hired and Controlled by the President of the U.S.A.*

"Color of Law" simply means that a person in a government official capacity, who holds the authority to implement the law, commits an illegal action under the appearance of authority, which exceeds such authority. Specifically, it is a violation of federal law for a lawful process to be perverted or used by a civil servant for an illicit purpose to intimidate, unduly burden, or harm another.

More specifically, it is a federal crime for anyone acting under "Color of Law" willfully to deprive or conspire to deprive a person of a right protected by either the Constitution or U.S. Statutory law.

In detail, a public servant violating Color of Law commits an offense if he/she intentionally subjects another to mistreatment or to arrest, detention, search, seizure, dispossession, assessment, or lien that he/she knows is unlawful or intentionally denies or impedes another in the exercise or enjoyment of any right, privilege, power, or immunity, knowing his/her conduct is unlawful.

# The 4<sup>th</sup> Amendment (Search & Seizure)

The 4<sup>th</sup> Amendment is an amendment to the United States Constitution and part of the Bill of Rights. It prohibits unreasonable searches and seizures and requires any warrant to be judicially sanctioned and supported by probable cause. It was adopted in response to the abuse of the writ of assistance, a type of general search warrant issued by the British Government and a major source of tension in pre-Revolutionary America. The 4<sup>th</sup> Amendment sets high standards to protect individuals inside their private property.

Should, however, a private residence transition into a commercial operation, then the standard for "reasonable" and "probable cause" becomes easier to meet, and falls under a commercial property standard, which is why Fire Marshalls have the authority to inspect shopping malls, churches, schools, etc.

Conversely, private property has a very high standard of protection against government authority, and each state has statutes that protect these property rights. Connecticut's private property statute is 47-1 (which goes back to the foundation of Connecticut in 1783).

# The Connecticut Freedom of Information Act (Government Disclosure)

*Federally Defined Civil Rights (Enforceable Rights Against Other Parties)*

It was only in 1975 that Connecticut passed its Freedom of Information Act, signed by Governor Ella Grasso (D). Nationally, it stood as one of the more aggressive renderings of its kind. Governor Grasso, the first female governor in America, took particular pride in Connecticut leading the charge in open governance.

As a young graduate of Trinity College in Hartford, Connecticut, I worked in Mrs. Grasso's administration in 1978 as the Governor's liaison to the towns to help rationalize, form, and launch cable television regional utility companies throughout the state. I met with her a few times in the governor's office, mainly about a matter that had transpired in Fairfield County, and found her to be a most serious advocate for the people's rights.

In her observations and directives, in a non-partisan manner, she respected the views and voices of each person (both democrat and republican town mayors, etc.) upon whom I reported. I believed that I had witnessed what a civil servant's center of gravity could indeed be.

Up until recently, the above was my only frame of reference for the Freedom of Information Act – FOIA - in Connecticut; it was something Ella Grasso championed.

I did not know the details but I knew this: if a person stood in conflict with any level of government, that the individual had the right to know what that government was saying and strategizing about that person.

Since then, apparently, government entities have been let off the hook by crying that this obligation to fetch records is too difficult, too time consuming, and too detailed in nature – causing them to simply say "no" to a requesting citizen.

This is what happened to me, so I am optimistic hoping that the F.B.I can weigh in on this topic as well, forcing The Town of Simsbury to release records.

From what I have read, though, it seems that there is no real penalty levied against a town if they deny information.

When a request is denied, the process is for the citizen to bring the situation to a judge. Only if the judge orders the town to open its records and, then, the town refuses, is there a backlash charge of contempt of court. Even then, as in one Stamford, Connecticut case where Stamford was found guilty of violating FOIA, the judge only applied a $300 fine and ordered compliance.

# Civil Rights

A civil right is an enforceable right or privilege, which if interfered with by another *gives rise to an action for injury (a law suit)*. Examples of civil rights are freedom of speech, press, and assembly; the right to vote; freedom from involuntary servitude; and the right to equality in public places.

Where does one start in digging into this topic?

First, as I have come to realize, professional magistrates, such as Mayor Mary, remain experts at clipping a person's civil rights wings while avoiding detection of doing so. With crimes such as murder, where a dead body lies on the street, it is a no-brainer: an investigation must be carried out as to whether a crime (murder) had been committed or whether an accidental or natural death was in play.

Conversely, with Civil Right violations, very few bits of prima facial evidence exist to which one can point; arguments consist of only claims of illegal treatment ... unless there is something on film, on tape, or in writing.

But even then, Civil Rights violations are not, strictly speaking, against the law. Instead, the law gives the victim the right to sue the perpetrator of the abuse. A Civil Right is the right to sue, not a right to have your nemesis prosecuted.

In the face of this legal murkiness, I might point out to the normal Americans out there – who simply know right from wrong - that from 2010-2013 ... the Town of Simsbury caused unwarranted infringement of my privacy and well-being, and repressed my ability to participate in the civil and political life of the community.

# Conclusion

---

Considering how slippery the law is in the Civil Rights and Freedom of Information domains, at first glance one may say their bearing on this case is, at best, weak. But even if these violations of law cannot be practically prosecuted, the violations nevertheless rise to the surface and support the conspiracy claims of the laws that happen to have teeth in them: Color of Law and $4^{th}$ Amendment violations.

Paramount to everything said, one recalls the Declaration of Independence and the U.S. Constitution which proclaim our *Natural Rights* to life, liberty and property. These rights sit above government reach unless criminal or commercial activity is involved. Through its behavior, the town demonstrated wanton disregard for the very underpinnings of The United States of America – and so far, has gotten away with it.

# End of Manuscript

*Below: Learning to fly – with my grandfather in 1953,
when it was still Government for the People*

Thanksgiving 1953 - 13 months -

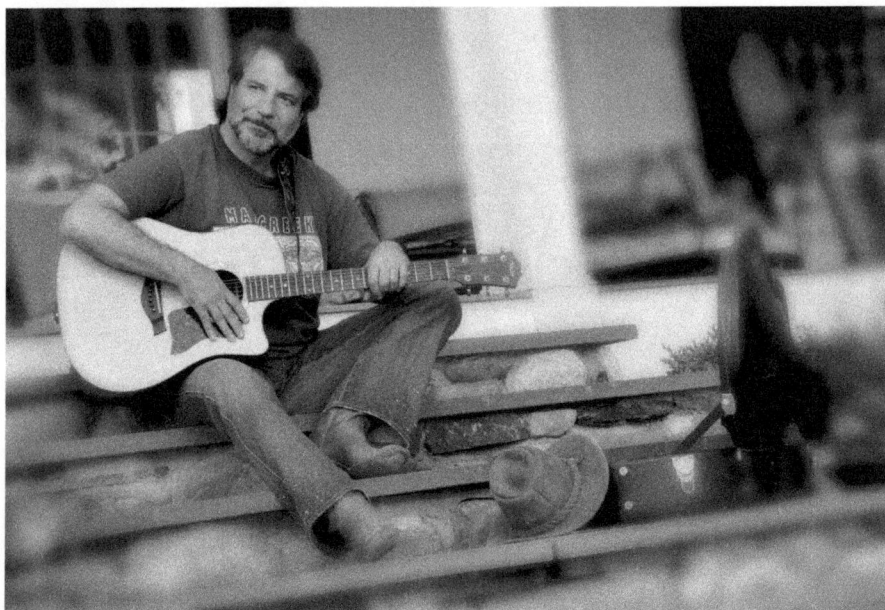

*The Author, on his West Simsbury porch*

www.ingramcontent.com/pod-product-compliance
Lightning Source LLC
Chambersburg PA
CBHW030302030426
42336CB00009B/494